wild
and free

wild
and free

stories chosen by
wendy cooling

Dolphin

A Dolphin Paperback

First published in Great Britain in 1997
by Orion Children's Books
a division of the Orion Publishing Group Ltd
Orion House
5 Upper St Martin's Lane
London WC2H 9EA

A catalogue record for this book is available
from the British Library
Typeset by Deltatype Ltd, Birkenhead, Merseyside
Printed in Great Britain by Clays Ltd, St Ives plc
ISBN 1 85881 461 8

contents

black tail

geoffrey malone

Black Tail sat upright and peered into the darkness. There was something wrong. He was sure of it. He had sensed it the moment his head broke the surface. It wasn't the dam – that had been the first thing he had checked.

There was something menacing out there in the forest.

He put his head on one side and listened. The first breeze of the dawn was feeling its way through the fir trees. It ruffled the pond and sent water slapping against the wooden sides of the lodge opposite. Wagami, his mate, would still be asleep. Her first litter of kittens was due at any time and she tired easily these days.

He felt a sudden tremor through his hind feet and heard the dam groan beneath him. It was thirty metres long and almost two metres high, stretching across the river like a bristling hedgerow. He and Wagami had built it last autumn, working night and day to have it ready in time. Afterwards, they had built their lodge, cutting branches to size, packing stones into the cracks and plastering it all over with thick mud. By the time the first November blizzard came howling out of the north, it had set like concrete. No animal, not even a grizzly bear, could tear its way in now. So long as the dam held they were safe. The only entrance to the lodge was deep below the surface, well away from their enemies.

Black Tail slipped down into the water and swam along the face of the dam. He noticed the level had risen a body's width since sunset, but at this time of year that was only to be expected. Everywhere, winter was in headlong retreat and rivers and lakes were swollen with melted snow. The forest was stirring with new life. And yet Black Tail was ill at ease. Again, he had that feeling of danger.

He stopped swimming and listened intently to the sounds of the forest. The raccoons were busy. The old male was squabbling with his family over some bird's eggs they had found. Black Tail turned his head and caught the scent of red fox. The vixen had been screaming earlier, demanding food from her mate. That meant her cubs had been born. He would warn Wagami.

And then he knew what was worrying him. It was the unmistakable smell of woodsmoke.

The discovery unsettled him. It was the wrong season for forest fires. Nothing could catch alight at this time of year. He worried about it for a while longer until the sound of a muffled bang deep inside the dam drove everything else from his mind.

He dived and found a branch being torn out of place by the sheer pressure of the water. Already, it had opened up a hole in the fabric of the dam. He steadied it between his massive front teeth, then, with strong little hands, began to thread it back into the bed of the stream.

Feverishly, Black Tail worked to repair the damage. He swam to the far bank and with his razor sharp teeth felled a tree twelve centimetres thick in less than ten minutes. He cut the branches into metre lengths. One at a time, he towed them to the dam and used them to brace the front wall. Next, he wedged smaller branches in between, then carried stones from the river bed tucked under his chin and plugged the remaining gaps with them. Finally, he gathered a mouthful of the smallest and juiciest branches and returned to the lodge.

Wagami greeted him with a low whistle as his head poked up inside the entrance hole. Black Tail climbed out and stood on the earth step below the main chamber to dry

himself. He gave her the fresh alder and she whistled again
in pleasure, licking his face and nuzzling him while he used
both hands to squeeze the water out of his pelt. Then they
sat together on the floor munching strips of bark and
rotating the branches like so many corn cobs. They licked
the sap from their fingers with appreciative little whoops
and grunts. When they had finished they groomed them-
selves, spreading the body oil beavers secrete deep into the
roots of their fur. This would keep their pelts water-
repellent and unmatted, and also protect them from the
icy cold.

Wagami showed him the soft bed of bark shavings she
was preparing for the kittens. Black Tail cleaned the main
chamber of twigs and the odd small pebble. Then he and
Wagami lay down back to back like dogs, enjoying each
other's warmth, and went to sleep.

In the world outside, the sun climbed higher and the
ground began to steam. The first mosquitoes of the year
danced together, hungry for blood. From some way above
the beaver's dam, the harsh scream of a blue jay ripped
through the forest. It came again and the forest fell silent,
listening to its warning. Alarmed, other birds began to join
in. Very soon every creature there knew that Man had
come.

Black Tail was finding it hard to sleep. He gave up trying,
slipped out of the lodge, swam out to the dam and
scrambled up. He was just about to run along the top of it
when something stopped him in his tracks. It was a strange
scent, one he had never met before. It was sweet and oily
and for some reason it made the hair stand up all along his
spine.

There was a shout. The beaver spun around in alarm and
saw the men. There were four of them, and they were

pointing at him. One of them was unslinging something from his shoulder. The next moment, he saw Wagami's head break the surface close to the lodge. A dog began to bark. Black Tail screamed at her to get back.

Then there was a loud bang and something hard smacked into the wood beside him. A shower of splinters covered his fur. There was another bang and a violent blow knocked him over. Head over heels he tumbled down the far side of the dam, where a clump of bushes broke his fall. His back leg felt numb and useless. He had to get away ... and fast! They were gaining on him. The dog was almost hoarse from barking. Black Tail could hear the men calling to one another as they crashed through the undergrowth after him.

His leg was a dead weight, dragging him back, but he knew the river was very close. Somehow, he got there first and felt the current seize hold of him and whirl him away. On either side, rocky cliffs grew higher. He became part of a smooth green wave that swooped and raced through a narrow gorge. Then water crashed over his head and he was seized in a fierce backwash that dragged him down and trapped him under an overhanging rock. He came to the surface spluttering and fighting for breath. It was the nearest he had ever come to drowning.

Much later, the river began to open out. The force of the water slowed and it grew shallow until it barely reached his underbelly. Half swimming, half stumbling, he pressed on, his wounded leg jarring on the pebbles. Ahead of him, in the middle of the river, he saw a jumble of rocks. It looked a good place to rest up. Then, when he had got his strength back, he would return and find Wagami.

At that moment, he heard the dog barking. If he could only reach the rocks there might just be a chance.

He almost made it. He was only a few metres short when

the dog reappeared. Black Tail heard the note of triumph in its bark and knew it had seen him. He was trapped. The dog was splashing towards him. And then he caught the musty smell of a Grizzly bear full in the face.

The bear was lying on a low, flat rock. Black Tail guessed it had been fishing: there were scales all round its mouth. It must have been asleep and the dog's barking had woken it up. Black Tail froze in horror.

Grumbling to itself, the Grizzly got to its feet and stood upright, blinking in the sunlight. It was fully grown and well over six foot tall, with claws four inches long.

The men had seen it too. They were shouting at the dog to come back. The bear heard them and snarled, the hair on its face puffing up in rage.

The dog only saw it at the last moment. It yelped in fright, tried to turn but lost its footing and fell sideways into the water. There was a sharp crack and the whine of a bullet passing overheard. The Grizzly bared its teeth and went in after the dog. There was another shot and two more in quick succession. Then the men lost their nerve and fled. One of them dropped the rucksack he had been carrying.

Black Tail watched the bear stoop and pick it up. It rummaged through the contents, then sat down on the bank. It had found something to eat. For the next couple of minutes, Black Tail heard it grunting in pleasure. Then it gave a loud yawn, got to its feet and walked quietly away on all fours. Only then did Black Tail move.

Wagami was distressed. She swam up and down in front of the lodge calling loudly for Black Tail. The men had been gone for some time and their scent had long since faded, yet there was still no sign of him.

As she swam, she felt a stabbing pain that made her groan

out loud. Deep inside her, the kittens were restless. Slowly, Wagami turned towards the lodge. She knew her time had come.

Towards the end of the afternoon, Black Tail found himself in a deep, smooth-moving river. There was a dull roaring in his ears, but he was hardly aware of it.

Too late, he realised what was happening. He tried to turn and swim for the bank but the river was accelerating and he was swept over the falls like a bundle of rags. Then, there was only thunder and spray and he was falling right into the middle of it.

The beaver was lying on a bank of pebbles at the water's edge with no memory of getting there. His entire body ached. His ribs hurt dreadfully whenever he tried to move. He licked his lips. They were dry and cracked.

He was drifting back to sleep when he heard human voices. His heart lurched and he started to struggle up. Pebbles were crunching underfoot. Getting louder. Coming towards him! He caught the hateful smell of Man and hissed in fear.

A shadow fell across him. He tensed, waiting for the blow, but none came. He stared up into the face of a boy with eyes as black as night. There was a bigger man behind him. Then everything went blank.

The next time he woke, he knew they had taken him back to their lodge. Their smell was everywhere. Rigid with fear, the beaver pretended to be dead. Time passed. Cautiously, he opened his eyes and saw he was surrounded by high wooden sides. He was lying on a thick bed of willow bark.

Carefully, Black Tail felt his bad leg and found it had been smeared with some strange fat. His nose wrinkled at the smell. It was still very sore but the worst of the pain had gone, and he felt very hungry.

The boy must have heard him moving. His face appeared, looking down at the beaver. His mouth opened and Black Tail shrank from the smell of human breath. Black Tail hissed at him.

A young aspen branch was dropped into the box. Black Tail looked at it with suspicion. Next, the boy set down a bowl of water. He went away, but the beaver knew he was waiting nearby.

He sat up and after a while picked picked up the branch, sniffed it and took a cautious bite. Then he was chewing hard, all the while flicking his ears from side to side keeping track of the men. When the boy dropped a piece of bark in front of him, Black Tail hissed and threatened him with his teeth. Then the delicious smell of maple sap filled his nostrils and he stretched out and touched it. He broke a piece off and nibbled it. Nothing had ever tasted so good. He ate the rest greedily and went back to sleep.

Black Tail made a rapid recovery, helped by the strange humans. They bore him no harm, but he still hissed at them whenever they came too close.

On the second night, he explored the cabin. The walls and floor were made of heavy logs and he tried to cut his way out, but the taste of creosote on the logs was unpleasant and burnt his mouth.

On the third night he was sniffing at the door when he leapt back in great alarm. There was a dog on the other side, growling at him. It growled all night long and Black Tail hissed back. The beaver's cries woke the humans.

'The little brother is well again,' the big man said the next night. 'The bullet wound is healed. Tomorrow, he will return and find his own people.'

The boy began to protest but his father held up a hand. 'We must do what is best for him. He is ready to leave.'

'But those hunters!' the boy exclaimed. 'If they see him again they'll kill him!'

The man gave a sad smile and shook his head. 'The Beaver People are wise,' he said. 'Once, they nearly all died because men wanted their fur. Now, they are strong again. He will remember all he has learnt. He will live. I promise you.'

At sunset the following evening, the man followed a game path that threaded its way in and out of the pine trees. Over his shoulder he carried a large sack. The boy walked behind, his head hung down.

When they reached the lake, the sun was slipping behind the tree tops, turning the water blood-red. A fish jumped for a fly, leaving an ever-widening circle of ripples behind. Carefully, the man laid the sack down. He opened it and stepped out of the way.

Without a backward glance, Black Tail slipped into the lake. He gave a wheeze of pleasure and was gone.

He travelled all night, keeping to the lakes and rivers wherever possible. Like all beavers, he was a slow mover on land and an easy prey for predators such as bobcats or bears.

Once, while crossing a neck of rock between two lakes, he met a timber wolf. The wolf was old and weak and only had its back teeth left. It was in no condition to take on a healthy beaver. Black Tail snarled at it and the wolf pretended to be following a rabbit scent instead.

By the end of the following day, he came to a muskeg swamp where the mosquitoes followed him in vicious, biting clouds. Almost blinded, he blundered on through the shallows until his coat was covered with the foul-smelling mud. But by now, he knew he knew he was close to home.

Driven on by the thought of Wagami, he climbed a steeply wooded hill and another one beyond that. And then, he was standing by a familiar rock looking down at their lodge. He suddenly noticed the height of the water behind the dam and his pleasure gave way to sudden anger. The level was dangerously high. It would soon flood the lodge or even burst open the dam itself. Where was Wagami?

He raced towards the water and swam out to the dam. The overflow channel was blocked. He tugged and pulled the debris of old branches clear and watched the water start to gush away. But still there was no sign of Wagami. Again, he called for her. Then he remembered the men and the dog and a terrible fear seized him. A little bubbling cry formed in the back of his throat. He dived for the entrance to the lodge and came up inside it in a sudden, noisy splash that terrified Wagami.

She was on her feet in an instant, spitting at him in fear. Her four helpless kittens began to whimper and this made her even more angry. Black Tail tried to reassure her but wisely made no attempt to come any closer. Later, she joined him by the dam and mewed in greeting, but it took another two days before she would allow him inside the lodge to meet his kittens. After that, Black Tail was busier than ever, bringing her water-weed and looking after them with her. As they played in the water, chasing each other, twisting and diving, happy to be together again, a magpie watched them. It saw something glinting in the sun and flew down to investigate. It was a brass cartridge case. The bird took it in its beak and flew in triumph to its nest in the old fir tree. The last trace of Man was gone.

wandering prince

gordon snell

The circus was quiet now. In the hazy moonlight, the big tent and the caravans looked like a group of huge, strange animals crouching in the field. An owl hooted in the forest nearby. The only other sound was a steady munching, as Prince the pony chewed the grass around the tree he was tied to.

Prince was pleased with himself: the evening's show had been a big success, and Prince was sure that he had been the star attraction. The audience clapped loudly when he came prancing in, with his red bridle and the spray of bright feathers on his head. They were delighted when he stood on his hind legs and walked round the ring, and when he trotted round and round with Laura, the acrobat, standing on one leg on his back.

He was sure they had liked him more than any of the other acts: more than Chapman the ringmaster, with his twirly moustaches, red coat and cracking whip; more than his daughter, Laura, swinging on the high trapeze or walking on the tightrope; more than Laura's husband, Dan, with his knife-throwing and sword-swallowing; more even than Bobo the Clown, who kept falling over and spilling buckets of water on himself; and certainly the audience liked him more than the only other animals in the show – Dilly and Dally, the Performing Pekinese. Prince thought they were very silly, with their fancy ribbons and their ladder-climbing act, and their yapping in time to music.

So, as he munched away at the grass in the moonlight, Prince looked forward to the two performances Chapman's Circus were going to give tomorrow at this little town beside the New Forest, and he smiled as he thought of the cheers and applause to come.

Suddenly Prince stopped munching, and lifted his head, listening. He had the feeling he was being watched. He turned, and saw a face gazing at him from the trees at the edge of the forest. It was another pony.

The two ponies stared at each other for more than a minute, without moving. Then the newcomer walked slowly out from the trees and across the field, towards Prince. He was one of the wild ponies that live in the New Forest, and he was brown and tough-looking, with a shaggy mane and tail that had clearly never been trimmed and groomed like Prince's. The Forest pony stopped a few yards away, and again the two of them stared at each other for a while. Then the Forest pony turned his head away, and began munching the grass. Prince didn't know quite what to do, so he started munching too, now and then glancing warily at the other pony.

'Where did you spring from, then?'

Prince was startled by the sudden, sharp question: but he didn't want to show it.

'Circus,' he said, trying to sound gruff.

The Forest pony grunted, and went on chewing the grass. After a couple of minutes he looked up and said, in the same challenging tone: 'What's your name, then?'

'Prince.'

'Prince, eh?' The Forest pony made a noise that sounded very like a chuckle of laughter. Prince was annoyed.

'What's yours?' he said, trying to sound bolder than he really felt.

The Forest pony stared at Prince for a bit, then said, 'Joe,' and went back to his chewing. Prince did the same. Then Joe spoke again.

'What do you do, in the circus?'

Prince could sense that behind the rather sneering tone of the question, Joe was really curious to know. He felt that here was his chance to get the upper hand.

'Oh, this and that,' he said, casually. 'I walk on my hind legs, as a matter of fact. I wear feathers on my head, and a red bridle. I trot round, balancing a lady on my back. I snatch the clown's hat and he chases me. Then I throw it into the audience ...'

Prince stopped. He could hardly believe his ears. Joe was laughing. Laughing at *him*. Prince was furious.

'What's so funny?' he snarled.

'You do all that?' asked Joe, still chuckling. 'Hind legs ... feathers ... balancing ladies ... throwing hats about ... ?'

'Certainly I do,' said Prince.

'Whatever for?'

The question completely stumped Prince. He had never asked himself *why* he did his circus act. He had never met anyone who *didn't* think it was clever – and now here was this scruffy character from the Forest, actually laughing with scorn at his skills.

'I bet you couldn't do all that,' said Prince, huffily.

'Wouldn't want to,' said Joe. 'I'd rather do pony-things, not silly tricks to amuse humans, like some performing dog.'

This really stung Prince's pride. Was Joe comparing *him* to idiotic creatures like Dilly and Dally? He snorted with rage – and the faint suspicion that Joe might perhaps be right made him angrier still. He snorted again, and pawed the ground, and charged, head down, at Joe. But the rope pulled him up, just out of range, and he stood there, pawing and snarling and baring his teeth.

'That's more like it!' said Joe. 'Now you're acting like a real pony!'

Prince stopped snarling, and his anger faded away. He

found he was rather pleased at Joe's approval. He tossed his head, and whinnied.

'Of course I'm a real pony,' he said. 'What did you think I was? A crocodile?' Joe laughed.

'Come on then, Prancing Prince,' he said. 'Let's go!'

Prince was taken aback.

'Go? Go where?' he asked.

'Into the forest, of course,' said Joe.

Prince didn't like the idea. The forest looked dark and threatening. But he couldn't admit that to Joe. Luckily, though, he had the perfect excuse.

'I'd love to go,' he said, 'but I can't. I'm tied to the tree.'

'No problem,' said Joe. 'What do you think teeth are for?' And he promptly started chewing at the rope.

'Wait,' said Prince. 'I don't really want … that is, I don't think we should …'

Joe was impatient.

'You want to get free, don't you? Well, start chewing!' He went on biting at the rope, and there was nothing Prince could do but start biting, too. It wasn't long before the rope began to fray, and soon only a thin thread connected one part of it to the other.

'Go on – now – pull!' said Joe.

Reluctantly, Prince pulled. The rope snapped. He was free. But did he really want to be? Prince wasn't at all sure.

'Come on then!' called Joe. 'Follow me!' And he trotted off into the shadowy trees of the forest. Prince looked around. He would have been quite pleased if Mr Chapman had come storming out of his caravan, swearing, and tied him up again. But the field was quiet, and there was no one to stop him going. If he stayed where he was, Joe would come back and mock at him. He couldn't bear that – so off he went, walking timidly into the forest.

All around him were tall trees. They seemed to Prince like

a crowd of giants, waiting and watching. A breeze stirred the leaves above his head, and the patterns of moonlight on the forest floor rippled like water. Somewhere among the shadows, an owl hooted. Prince's hoofs made a crunching noise as he walked on the dry brushwood and leaves. Some way ahead he could see the dark shape of Joe, who had stopped and was looking back at him.

'Come on,' said Joe, and he started trotting, on a zigzagging path among the trees. Prince followed: he didn't want to lose sight of Joe, so he dodged and darted behind him through the Forest, with the branches brushing against him.

Joe stopped, and Prince came to a halt beside him, panting. They were at the edge of the trees now, looking out on to a stretch of heathland, with a rough carpet of heather and clumps of bushes here and there. After the gloom of the forest, the heath was silvery bright in the moonlight.

Prince was thankful: he'd be glad to be out in the open again. But then he saw there was a fence between them and the heath. There was a five-barred wooden gate in it, nearly as high as Prince's neck; and the gate was closed.

'Ready to jump?' asked Joe.

At first, Prince thought he must be joking. The only jumps he had ever made were in the circus, when Bobo the Clown held a pole out for him, a foot or so above the ground. This gate must be over three times as high. But Joe was serious.

'Up and over, Prince!' he said – and he rushed towards the gate, leapt into the air, and landed on the far side. He looked back at Prince.

'Come on, it's easy,' he said, 'and more fun than capering about in that circus.'

Prince walked slowly back, away from the gate, and then

turned. He took a deep breath, and charged. The gate loomed up in front of him. He closed his eyes and pushed his back feet hard on the ground, reaching up, up into the air with his front legs. For a moment, he seemed to be flying like a bird: it was a marvellous feeling. Then the ground was rushing up towards him, and his front feet landed with a thud. He stumbled, recovered his balance, and stood still. He lifted his head in the air and whinnied with delight and relief. He'd done it!

Joe whinnied, too.

'Nice work,' he said. 'I never thought you'd make it.'

'Whatever made you think that?' said Prince. He felt very proud of himself – but things didn't turn out to be quite as easy as he expected …

'What next?' he asked Joe.

'Racing,' said Joe. 'Bet you can't catch me!' He began to trot, and then to canter, across the heath. Prince managed to keep up with him for a couple of minutes, but he was getting tired. A short spell of trotting was all he was used to in the circus.

'I'm not as fit as I ought to be,' he thought to himself. 'Must try to get more exercise in future …'

'Away we go!' shouted Joe, and now he began to gallop over the heath, towards a wood on the far side. Prince pounded after him, but the gap between them was getting bigger. Joe must have been more than a hundred yards away when Prince saw him reach the wood and go galloping on into the trees. Panting heavily, he got to the place where Joe had gone into the wood. All he could see was a maze of leaves and shadows. Which way had Joe gone? Prince peered into the wood, and listened. He could hear nothing. The trees seemed simply to have swallowed Joe up. Prince was worried. If he went in there, he might get lost and never find his way out again. If he went back across

the heath, would he ever find the gate they had jumped –
let alone be able to jump back over it again? And even if he
did that, how would he find his way back through the dark
forest? Prince was miserable. He just stood there, not
knowing what to do.

Suddenly the silence was broken by a sound that nearly
made him jump into the air with fright. It was a sort of
grunting, wailing roar, and it sounded anything but
friendly. He turned round. There on the heath, just a little
distance away, was a huge creature with a tall head, and
antlers like mad, spiky television aerials. It was a red deer.
Behind him Prince could see a group of smaller deer, some
grazing, others looking up to see what their leader was
making such a row about.

The big deer roared again, then put his head down, and
started running towards Prince.

Then Prince had an idea. He stood up on his hind legs,
just like he did in the circus. Then he lifted his head and
neighed loudly.

The big deer stopped in his tracks, like a car screeching to
a halt. He looked up at Prince, and his mouth dropped
open in amazement.

Prince was still scared: he couldn't walk on his hind legs
for all that long. He'd have to come down soon, and what
would the deer do then? The big creature was still staring at
him. Just as Prince felt that he'd have to give up, he heard a
voice behind him. It was Joe.

'It's all right, Thunderhead, he's a friend of mine.'

'Well, tell him he shouldn't dance about like that – it's
not natural,' said Thunderhead, and he walked away.

'Sorry I wasn't around when he showed up,' said Joe, 'I
thought you were following me into the wood. Then when
I stopped, and you weren't there, I came back to find you.'

'Thanks,' said Prince. 'I couldn't have stood up like that for much longer.'

'You must teach me that trick – it could come in useful.'

'I'd be pleased to.'

Prince was delighted to have Joe's approval.

'Now, let me show you around a bit more,' said Joe. 'There's lots we haven't seen yet.' They walked together into the wood.

The dawn was coming now, and the dark shapes of the trees were beginning to get back their daylight colours. The air was cool and fresh, and full of delicious smells, quite different from the circus smells Prince was used to: sawdust, and canvas, and leather, and diesel fumes from the trucks and the generator. Here in the wood, the soft breeze carried the scents of many flowers, and there was a clean, damp smell from the old leaves scattered on the ground.

They came to a busy stream, and waded in and drank the cold, refreshing water. Crossing the stream, they came out of the wood into a wide field of grass, and galloped around it, just for the joy of running. They rolled about on the grass, kicking their legs in the air. Then they lay down and dozed in the sunshine.

'The circus!' he said. 'I'll be late for the afternoon show!' He nudged Joe, who woke up, blinking in the sunlight.

'Joe – I've got to get back to the circus.'

'Why?'

Prince found the question hard to answer.

'Well … they'll be expecting me. I'll be late …'

'Let them wait,' said Joe. 'And anyway, why go back at all? It's a good life here. Stay in the forest. I've got so much to show you.'

Prince felt a glow of pleasure: Joe wanted to be his friend. He would like to say yes, he'd stay. But could he really leave the circus, and all the applause, and the travelling from place to place? Then Prince realised that although he'd travelled all over the country, he'd really *seen* very little: just fields that were very much alike, and the same circus tent, and the inside of the rattly old horsebox he travelled in. In fact, he'd seen more and learned more in his few hours in the forest with Joe than he had in all his travels with Mr Chapman. And yet …

'I'd better go, Joe,' he said, sadly. 'They'll come out looking for me, and *make* me go back.'

'Well, if that's how you feel, there's not much I can do about it.' Joe sounded hurt. 'Come on.'

Joe led the way back through the wood and across the heath. This time he gave no words of praise when Prince managed to jump the gate again. Back they went, through the forest trees, saying nothing. They stopped at the edge of the forest, and looked at the field with the circus tent in it. There was a lot of activity going on now – music was playing, and Bobo the Clown was standing outside the tent, ringing a bell, and shouting: 'Roll up! Roll up!'

Just then, Mr Chapman and Laura came round the side of the tent. Mr Chapman was shouting angrily.

'Ten minutes to go, and still no sign of him! I should never have let *you* tie him up! Now look what's happened! No pony!'

'I tied him up all right,' said Laura tearfully. 'But he chewed through the rope …'

'From now on we'll put him on a chain,' said Mr Chapman. '*And* I'll cut his rations!'

Prince nearly turned round right then – but he noticed that Laura was crying. She had always been fond of him, and petted him, and given him lumps of sugar. The rest of them couldn't care less, thought Prince: to them, he was just a stupid pony that did tricks and helped to bring in the money. He didn't want Laura to take the blame.

Prince made up his mind: he had a plan all worked out now. He said to Joe:

'Come and see the show tonight. There's a narrow gap in the tent at the back there, and you can peep through.'

'I might,' said Joe.

'Please do – *please*. It's important.'

'Okay,' said Joe. 'It'll be a chance to say goodbye, anyway.'

Yes, thought Prince. Tonight, after the show, the circus would pack up and move off to somewhere miles away.

Joe turned and walked off into the forest. Prince watched him go. Then he walked smartly out into the circus field.

'There he is!' shouted Mr Chapman, grabbing Prince roughly by his mane. 'Where have you been, you four-legged fool? I'll teach you to go running off like that!' And he gave Prince a slap on the side of his head.

'Don't!' said Laura.

'Get that beast's bridle on at once! We've only two minutes before the show starts!'

He went stamping off, and Laura put on Prince's red bridle with the feathers on top. Usually, he felt good in it – but now he thought it made him look rather foolish.

Prince went through all his tricks as usual, and the audience clapped and cheered. But he found that he didn't like the sound much, any more. He was thinking of the sound the birds made, in their dawn chorus in the wood, and the sound of the splashing stream, and the sound of his hoofs, and Joe's, as they crunched the dry forest floor.

When the afternoon show had finished, Mr Chapman said: 'Right! Lock that pony in his horsebox! I'm not having him escaping again.'

So Prince spent the two hours until the next show standing in his cramped, dark box.

At the evening show he trotted round obediently as

usual, while Mr Chapman cracked his whip. Then, up he went on his hind legs, and pranced about, while the audience clapped. He glanced towards the gap in the far side of the tent, and there was Joe's face, gazing in.

No one in the circus tent was ready for what happened next. Prince started walking slowly towards Chapman. He backed away.

'That's enough, Prince – good boy, Prince,' he said nervously.

Prince leaned forward and snatched the whip out of his hand. He chewed on it, and the handle broke into pieces. Prince dropped them on the sawdust floor, and bowed. The audience laughed and clapped loudly: they thought this was part of the act. But Mr Chapman didn't laugh: he was snarling.

'Get out! The act's over! Get out of the ring!'

Prince took no notice. He reached his mouth up towards Mr Chapman's head, and snatched with his teeth, grabbing the ringmaster's black hair. The hair came away – the whole lot of it! It was a wig. Mr Chapman stood there with his bald head gleaming under the bright lights. The audience were delighted. They shouted and clapped and stamped their feet.

Mr Chapman, his face red with rage, made a grab at Prince, who started to trot round the ring with Mr Chapman chasing him. Prince's pace got quicker as the ringmaster panted along behind him. Then, he stopped suddenly, and rose on his hind legs; Mr Chapman ran straight into him, and fell over. The crowd cheered.

Prince took a bow, trotted out of the tent and round to the back, where Joe was.

'Come on!' said Prince. As they trotted away together into the forest, Prince glanced back and saw Mr Chapman in the entrance to the tent, shouting and shaking his fist.

Behind him stood Laura, smiling. She gave a goodbye wave.

The ponies ran through the forest, crashing against branches as they went. They jumped the gate, and ran out on to the heath, the way they'd come the night before. They ran into the wood on the far side, and then stopped and listened. All they could hear was the rustle of leaves in the night breeze, and the far-off hooting of the owl. No one seemed to be following.

They smiled at each other.

'That was quite a show!' said Joe admiringly.

'It wasn't bad, was it, for a farewell performance?' said Prince.

'You're not going back, then?' asked Joe.

'Never!' said Prince. 'I'm retiring from the circus! This is the life for me!' And he lay on the ground and kicked his legs in the air for sheer joy. Then he felt something between his head and the ground, and realised he still had his bridle on. He sat up, dismayed.

'The bridle!' he said to Joe. 'I can't go round the forest with this on my head, and the feathers too. It looks ridiculous. Help me get it off.'

With Prince telling him what to do, Joe began to pull at the buckles and straps with his teeth. Finally, the bridle slipped off and fell on the ground. Prince tossed his head and shook himself. He was free.

'Thanks, Joe.'

'It's a pleasure. Welcome to the forest.'

In reply, Prince raised his head and gave a loud whinny. Joe whinnied back. Then Prince picked up the bridle in his teeth, and hung it on the low branch of a tree.

The two ponies walked slowly away through the wood, in the dappled moonlight. Prince turned once, and looked back at the bridle, hanging in the tree. The coloured feathers made it look as if some strange, bright bird had perched there.

one, two, many

mary rayner

Charlie was a black cat, stately in his walk, quiet. And big. When he sat in your lap, you knew he was there. He had come to the house as a stray, fetched from a village some miles away where an elderly couple had taken him in.

'Oh, you won't need that,' they'd said, eyeing the cat box his new owners had with them. 'He'll sit in your lap in the car.'

And so he did, flinching a little at the oncoming headlights, but staying quite still otherwise until they reached his new home. Once there, he hid behind the sofa for two days and then came out and cautiously made friends.

He soon made the house his own, though he never came to terms with the cat flap. He preferred to have doors opened for him, and would miaow outside the kitchen window to be let in. Wherever it was that he had lived before, there had been no cat flaps. In Charlie's book, doors opened for you meant that humans cared.

It took him a while longer to be master of the garden. Neighbouring cats had been having the run of it for years, but Charlie fought them all. He steered clear of the truly terrifying black tom with the white feet, known far and wide as White Toes, but it was not long before White Toes discovered the cat flap and regularly helped himself to Charlie's dinner.

One night Charlie wandered out for a bedtime snack to his food saucers in the outhouse and caught White Toes licking the bowl clean. The shameless thief chased Charlie up his own stairs, but up in the attic Charlie turned and fought back with real fury.

In the morning there were bits of black and white fur everywhere, and Charlie had a deep gash down his neck, but White Toes was, from then on, more wary. Charlie saw him crossing the garden now and again, head down, battered ears flat to his head, keeping a watchful eye on the house.

Charlie spent his time sitting on window sills looking out, or curled up asleep, or making a stately tour of the garden. He was pleased that now it was all his. Life had never been so good. But his happiness was shortlived.

His new owners decided that he needed company. Chancing to hear of a litter of Burmese kittens ready for sale, they asked for one.

When she arrived, Charlie thought the new kitten was something else. She was skinny, and long-tailed, and a smoky cream colour, and her voice was like no cat Charlie had ever come across. It was not only loud and deep, it was unceasing. Her miaows filled the house from dawn to dusk. And she didn't sit on window sills or lie curled up. She climbed onto the mantelpiece in the kitchen, she balanced along the top of the dresser, she leapt from shelf to shelf bringing plates and cups down with her.

She was not polite to the owners of the house. She shouted at them for food in a way which Charlie thought shocking, and he told her so.

'D'you think?' She turned her pointed face towards him and opened her green eyes wide. 'But it works! You should try it.'

'Hrrumph,' said Charlie, and he walked his stately walk to the saucer in the outhouse.

The new kitten dashed after him, beat him to the saucer and skidded to a halt. 'There are mice!' she said excitedly. 'I can smell them. Have you caught any, Charlie?'

'Er, no,' said Charlie. 'Live and let live, that's my motto.'

'Oh Char*lie*. Don't be so silly. That's what we're here for.'

The very next day she caught her first mouse, and brought it proudly to the owners' feet.

'Clever girl!' they said. 'Charlie, you've been slacking.'

'You see?' she said to Charlie. 'Come on, come outside, I'm going to climb the tree.'

She lifted the cat flap easily, jumped through and dashed across the lawn. Charlie followed her awkwardly through the cat flap. It was a long time since he had done any running. He lumbered after her and flung himself at the big tree. She was already in the top branches.

About six feet up the trunk, Charlie got stuck. He clung there, feeling silly. Then he lowered himself backwards onto the grass, and sat licking his paws. His claws hurt from the strain of hanging on.

The owners laughed at him. 'Charlie, you should lose some weight!'

As the summer went by, in spite of himself Charlie became friends with the Burmese kitten. The owners called her Holly. Charlie and Holly curled up together during the day, and slept in the basket in the kitchen at night. Charlie allowed her to pounce on his tail, and simply cuffed her when she was too cheeky.

Winter passed. Holly was growing up, and beginning to take an interest in other cats. Charlie was a fixed cat, and could be no more than an uncle to her, but one evening White Toes came and sang to her through the kitchen window.

Holly tried to get out through the glass. She thought White Toes was the most romantic thing she had ever laid eyes on.

Charlie was disgusted. 'You can do better than that. You are a pedigree cat. White Toes is a thief and a vagabond. Look at his torn ears and scarred face. He has me to thank for some of those scars,' he added, looking at the floor with modest pride.

'I like him,' said Holly. 'He says I'm pretty.'

'You are, you are,' said Charlie. Why had he never thought to mention it?

Holly's owners took swift action. They too had noticed White Toes, and they had other plans for Holly.

Holly went away in the cat box, and Charlie found himself once more the only cat. He fitted in a lot more sleeping, and nobody pounced on his tail. It was wonderfully peaceful, but gradually he realised that he missed her.

Holly came back after a few days. She was in love. She had spent the days with a handsome young Burmese, and she could talk of no one else. Charlie listened, but after a while his eyes closed and his head nodded. Holly didn't notice, she just talked on.

The spring passed. Charlie was still master of the house and garden, though there were now the two of them. White Toes was no longer interested in Holly, he did not come and sing again. Holly lay about under the gooseberry bushes in the shade, stopped climbing trees, and was nowhere near so noisy. But she still caught mice.

And then one morning, very early, when Charlie was still dozing in the kitchen, he heard a lot of to-ing and fro-ing from the owners overhead. He paid little attention, but then it dawned on him that his breakfast had been forgotten. That *was* worrying.

He stretched, and went to find the owners to remind them. He found the female one in the room across the passage from the kitchen. Holly was there as well, in a large cardboard box. He could just see her ears. He approached her, but she stood up and hissed at him.

Charlie left the room hurriedly. There were squeaks –

tiny mews – coming from the box. This was no place for a male cat to be.

He climbed on to his lookout window sill in the outhouse and thought. First there had been one cat. Himself. Then two. Himself and Holly. Try as he might, Charlie could not count further. Now there were – one, two – many, he said to himself helplessly.

Over the following weeks he found out that there were indeed many. At first Holly and her kittens were locked away in the room across from the kitchen, and troubled him little. Even when Holly was treated to special food, fresh fish and liver, Charlie wasn't too bothered. He munched through his rubbery tinned food, thinking 'live and let live'.

But soon the kittens were brought into the kitchen. Humans crooned over them, Holly purred. They were picked up and cuddled. No one even gave Charlie a glance. He would have given anything to have Holly pounce on his tail or race him to the tree, but she was too busy nursing her kittens.

And there were, it seemed to Charlie, a huge number of them, all slant-eyed, all exactly the same pale cream as their mother. One had a kink in its tail but otherwise you couldn't tell them apart. One, two, many, muttered Charlie, walking his stately walk out to yet another bowl of tinned rubber. The female owner cooked scrambled egg and rice for the kittens, but when Charlie rubbed against her ankles to let her know that he'd like some too, she kicked him aside.

The kittens grew larger and stronger. Soon the biggest of them was bullying the others, pushing them out of the way so that he could get at his mother's milk. He bit their ears until they squeaked with pain and moved over. The female owner nicknamed him Genghis Khan, and stroked his fat tummy.

Charlie watched gloomily from across the kitchen.

'Poor old Charlie,' she said. 'You don't think much of Genghis Khan and the Mongol hordes, do you?'

Too right I don't, thought Charlie, marching out to check that at least the garden was still his. Where's it all going to end, that's what I'd like to know? He seriously considered murder, but put it to one side. Live and let live, he told himself.

One night, when Charlie was curled up fast asleep on the top landing, White Toes let himself into the house once more through the cat flap, and ate some of Holly's special food. No one saw him come or go, but when Holly went to her saucer in the morning she smelt the lingering traces of an intruder.

That day she carried every single one of her kittens, bump, bump, bump, up the stairs to her owners' bed.

From then on the special food was not left down, and the kittens were kept in the upstairs attic at night. But during the day they were everywhere.

They jumped on Charlie from the sofa, leapt out at him from behind doors and woke him up when he was asleep. Their mother was tireless. When she wasn't cleaning them or feeding them, she was out catching mice which she brought home so that they would learn to hunt. And not only mice. More than once Charlie's snoozes were disturbed by the female owner's shrieks when she found a live frog in the kitchen, and once Holly even brought in a grass snake.

'Why don't *you* catch things for them?' she asked Charlie.

'Hrrumph,' said Charlie.

He felt old and very tired. He went to sit on his high window sill in the outhouse, the kittens could not reach him there. He closed his eyes. He could still hear their shrill mews. They were as noisy as their mother had been. Noisier. And Genghis Khan had the hoarsest, loudest, worst voice of all.

But then something odd happened. When the kittens were three months old, a strange human came to the house and one of the kittens was put into a cat basket and taken away. Charlie saw it go. He sat on his window sill and struggled to make sense of what happened. The Mongol hordes must be fewer by one. But there were still many. A great many. Subtraction was beyond him.

Over the next few weeks it happened again. A lady came in a big car, and carried away two of the kittens, and a small boy with his mother took another. Many take away two, thought Charlie, and then another. Many take away many. You'd think that should leave none?

But there were *still* many. No getting away from it. The remaining kittens climbed up the curtains, fought savage battles with the tassels of the kitchen rug and clambered up on to the table to steal food.

Even Holly began to look weary. She took to climbing up on to the kitchen mantelpiece to get away from them, and snapped at them if they bothered her for milk when she was snoozing.

Twice more, kittens were fetched away. Charlie noted that only the one with the kink in its tail, and the big one, Genghis Khan, were left. Just me and Holly soon, he thought hopefully, walking his stately walk to sit at the top of the garden steps and keep watch.

Next day Kinky Tail went to a new home. Holly didn't seem to mind. She was curled up in the big chair with

Genghis Khan, who was, Charlie noticed, at least as big as she was. Not long now, thought Charlie.

Genghis Khan tried to make friends with Charlie. He had no brothers and sisters to play with. He rolled over in front of Charlie, lay on his back and waved his paws in the air. He made pretend dabs at Charlie's face, but Charlie wasn't having any. He turned his face away, stood up and walked off, waving a stately tail. I'll be rid of him soon, thought Charlie.

But Genghis Khan was not fetched away by anyone. He stayed, and he grew larger. Charlie could not believe it when, at feeding time, Holly stood back from the saucer and let him eat first.

'Why are you so soft with him?' he demanded.

A faraway look came into Holly's eyes. 'Because he's the image of his father. And he's got his father's marvellous voice.'

'Hrrumph,' said Charlie.

The female owner was just as bad. 'You soppy thing,' she said when Genghis rolled over at her feet, and she bent to stroke his chest. At night, when Charlie and Holly were turned out of the warm bedroom to sleep on the cold landing, she let Genghis stay and sleep on the bed.

'There is no justice,' said Charlie, stomping angrily up the garden steps. He marched across the lawn, past the big tree, and over to the lilac bush. And then all his fur rose on end. There was no mistaking that telltale scent. White Toes was back.

Charlie hurried indoors and spent that night on the top landing, but he slept badly, every sound made him jump. Next morning, when it was time for them all to be fed, Charlie made it clear to the owners that he wanted human protection while he ate. He kept looking nervously behind him at the cat flap, and ran after them when they left the outhouse, even though he hadn't finished eating.

He spent the day keeping a lookout for White Toes from his high window sill.

That evening, the thing he dreaded happened. White Toes came in through the cat flap, and swung over to the food saucers. Charlie jumped down. 'Keep off,' he hissed.

White Toes stood his ground.

This is it, thought Charlie, nothing else for it.

He went in to attack. They fought and bit and scratched, round and round the outhouse. Saucers were knocked flying, milk spilt. White Toes leapt onto the ironing board, Charlie after him. The ironing board toppled over sideways.

White Toes sprang clear and turned to face Charlie. They grappled together. Charlie felt a stinging slash across his eye and staggered back. White Toes banged out through the cat flap.

Charlie spent a long night up on his window sill, staring with his good eye out into the dark. The other was half shut. White Toes did not come back, but by morning Charlie's face was throbbing and he felt ill. He retired up to the bedroom.

It was a good twenty-four hours before anyone noticed his swollen face and the gash over his eye. The female owner put him in the cat box and drove him to the vet.

The vet was surprised at how still Charlie kept on the white table while he was examined. 'Hello, you've been in the wars,' he said, and then, to the female owner, 'and facing the enemy. No back or tail wounds. Quite a hero.'

Charlie felt himself held firmly, and then there was a sharp jab between his shoulders. He gave a low miaow, but did not struggle against the antibiotic injection.

'What a good fellow,' said the vet, rubbing his head.

Charlie felt proud.

At home, he stepped stiffly out of the cat box. Holly and Genghis licked his face. Charlie winced, but he allowed them to curl up against him. He hadn't the strength to jump up on to his high window sill.

Each morning the food saucers were licked ominously clean. White Toes was coming and going as if he owned the house. Charlie just wasn't well enough to take him on, and White Toes knew it.

Then one day he grew too confident. He swaggered in through the cat flap in broad daylight and surprised Genghis at his breakfast.

Genghis whipped round. Faced suddenly with an intruding tom, all his instincts took over. All those pretend battles with his brothers and sisters, all those fights with rug tassels and pouncings on his mother's tail were only a preparation for this. His fur bristled, his thin tail fluffed out to double its size, his big ears went flat, his mouth opened in a snarl. Out of it came the most terrible deep, growling singsong, unlike anything you have ever heard. It rose and fell in a sound to freeze your blood. He danced sideways on stiff legs towards White Toes.

In all his years of cat battles White Toes had never heard anything like it. He was not to know that this white-cream ball of fighting fur was a complete beginner, all he heard was the noise. What was this animal? Imagine coming face to face with a panther in your kitchen and you will know how White Toes felt. He stood rigid.

And in that instant Genghis struck. He flew at him, bowled him over, and seized his big square head in his front paws. With his back feet he pummelled White Toes's soft belly, scoring deep wounds with his long claws. White Toes screeched, and rolled free. He was back on his feet in a trice, and fled out through the cat flap.

Its crash brought Holly and Charlie hurrying to the outhouse. Genghis's bristling fur and still-flattened ears told them who had been there.

'Brave boy,' said Holly.

Genghis's coat was slowly smoothing down as he walked angrily round the cat flap, sniffing. 'He'd better not try that again,' he said.

The three cats went into the warm kitchen. Charlie lay down and Holly put her face against his and licked it. 'Ow,' said Charlie, but not very loud. She curled up against him. He put a paw over her, and his eyes closed.

Genghis came over, and slipped down beside his mother. He gave each cat's face a lick, then laid his head on his paws. Charlie did not move, and the three of them slept all day together. One, two, many, thought Charlie as he dozed off to the sound of Holly's purring. Not such a bad number after all.

a crazy dog

diana pullein-thompson

Go on, I'm giving her to you.' Jan Woods handed the three-month-old puppy to his friend, Mick Baker. 'Nobody wants her because she's black and grey instead of black and white and she's got too many spots.'

The puppy ran her healthy, bright pink tongue over Mick's shaven head.

'Here, take this,' continued Jan, handing Mick a rope with a ring at one end, 'Noose it round her neck, use it like a choker.'

So Mick took the puppy, whom he called Misty, back to his third floor flat in a tower block. He gave her a piece of bread and a bowl of water, shut her in the tiny kitchen and went off to see his friend about his next job, which was a burglary.

Misty, who had been one of five puppies, was lonely and afraid. She paced up and down, wondering whether Mick would ever return. The garage, in which she had lived until now, was cold and spartan, but it had smelt of her mother and was home. This kitchen smelt of disinfectant and very faintly of Mick.

Soon, Misty started barking, and once she started she couldn't stop. The barks were bigger than she was. She barked for her mum and for her beautiful black and white brothers and sisters. She barked because she was afraid and wanted company and because her body and her mind ached for exercise and space. When Mick came back at one o'clock in the morning she was hysterical with relief. She jumped up and licked his ears and whimpered with joy, for now she was ready to be loyal to him for life.

Every morning Mick crawled out of bed at about ten. He

gave Misty two slices of bread from a sliced loaf, ate a bowl of cereal, drank coffee, smoked a cigarette and then walked Misty round the block. In the afternoon he usually took her with him to see friends, and in the evenings she was left in the kitchen until he came home; then she slept with him on his large double bed.

Mick taught Misty to come when called, to catch balls and to sit when told. He also encouraged her to use the newspaper he spread on the kitchen floor as her lavatory.

Six months after Misty came to live with Mick, two burly policemen broke into the flat. They searched drawers and cupboards, while Misty barked at them wildly – for it seemed to her that they were breaking up her home. Shouting at her to be quiet, they collected together two boxes of silver spoons, three rings, a necklace, a camera, a marble clock and a silver hunter watch.

'We've got him this time,' the taller one said. 'If the fingerprints match up he'll get a long prison sentence.' Then Misty barked with relief as she heard Mick's footsteps on the concrete stairs.

'Stop that!' he told her, opening the door. 'Or we'll have the neighbours complaining.'

Once again Misty threw herself at Mick, whimpering with joy. But next moment the policemen, who had been hiding, jumped on him. They pushed him to the ground while Misty nipped their ankles. They slipped handcuffs round his wrists and led him away, slamming the door in Misty's face as she tried to follow.

Frightened, she spent the night on Mick's bed. In the morning she howled, until the howls took control of her and she couldn't stop. She heard someone shouting, a motorbike roaring away, a bus in the distance, but no more footsteps on the concrete stairs.

At last at lunch time Mick's friend, Tracey, came and

took Misty to a flat which she shared with her mother, Ching, the chow, and a cat called Fluffy.

'Go away, sheepdog,' snarled Ching, drawing back her lips. 'This is MY place.'

'Out, out!' hissed Fluffy arching her back.

'Sit!' said Tracey, before opening a tin of dog food and filling a bowl with water. 'There now. I expect you're hungry. Get away, Ching.'

When Misty had wolfed down the dog meat and drunk a whole bowl of water, Tracey went back to work and Misty started to circle the cat who spat at her.

'Stop that!' barked Ching. 'Or I shall bite you to bits,' and she opened her mouth wide so that Misty could see her sharp white teeth and purple tongue.

'I can't,' barked Misty. 'My legs won't stop.'

'I'll scratch your eyes out. I'll tear you apart,' hissed Fluffy.

Then Tracey's mother, who was plump as a cushion, with eyes like blue marbles, came into the flat, grabbed Misty and slapped her. 'You leave our Fluffy alone or I'll throw you out in the street,' she shouted. And the cat jumped on to her rescuer's shoulder and purred and purred.

'Stupid sheepdog,' snarled Ching.

'I'm not a sheepdog. I'm a collie,' panted Misty, her long tongue hanging out like pink salami.

'Same thing,' snapped Ching, before curling up in her basket, 'and now shut up. I want to sleep.'

'For Pete's sake stop running about, you daft dog,' cried Tracy's mother. 'You're enough to drive the sanest person mad. Why Tracey took up with that man, heaven alone knows. He's twisted as a corkscrew.'

But Misty was crazy with worry. Where was Mick? If he had gone for good who would look after her?

When Tracey came home she took Misty for a walk on a lead and Misty, who was looking for Mick, pulled until Tracey's arms ached and her patience snapped and she hit Misty across the nose. And then Misty's legs wanted to run and run, until she was so tired she would collapse and fall asleep. But Tracey dragged her back to the flat and shut her in the kitchen with a blanket to sleep on. Here Misty paced up and down like a tiger in a cage, her nerves raw as uncooked meat. She longed for the warm bed and Mick's body next to hers. Her tummy was upset and when Tracey's mother came to make an early morning cup of tea, she was outraged to see Misty had used the floor as a lavatory.

'You filthy dog,' she screamed. 'Get out!'

And she grabbed Misty by the collar, opened the flat door and kicked her down the stairs.

The door at the bottom was open, so Misty ran straight out and only just missed being hit by a car. And her legs kept running. They took her down streets, across roads and, at last, into a large green park where she paused for breath. The next moment a golden retriever dog joined her.

'You smell nice,' he said. 'Where's your owner? Mine's that woman waving an umbrella. She's lonely and fat and needs an awful lot of petting to keep her happy.'

'Mine's gone. Men came and took him away,' replied Misty.

'He was bad then,' the retriever said.

'No, he was good,' snapped Misty, 'the best.'

'He can't have been if he never took you in a park,' replied the retriever, beginning to sniff a tree.

'How do you know that?' asked Misty.

'When you came in your eyes were full of wonder. I know everything,' boasted the retriever. 'Must go. Bossyboots is calling again. Humans! They always want their own way.

But still we can't help loving the poor dears, can we? Take care. Look out for cars.'

When the retriever had gone Misty ran and ran, and, for the first time in her life, revelled in her speed. She drank from a pond, ate pieces of chicken and chips – remains of a takeaway meal thrown in a bin – and rolled in the grass. Later she came upon a railway station and watched the trains coming in. How big they were, how powerful! How wonderful to control them! Soon a fantasy grew in her head like a fever. Dodging the waiting passengers, she rushed forward biting wildly at the trains as they arrived, imagining that they stopped and started at her command.

When night fell she found a cosy hollow on the railway embankment and, tired at last, slept until dawn. Next morning she was back at the station, dodging everyone who tried to catch her.

'What do you think you're doing?' asked a prancing poodle, who was blueish white like skimmed milk.

'Controlling the monsters,' panted Misty, tail up, tongue out.

'You should be on a lead, not a jewel-studded one like mine, of course, but a brown leather one,' said the poodle.

'Too busy to talk. Look, there's another monster, coming in on the other line!' panted Misty before rushing over the bridge to platform 2.

'Stop that dog,' a passenger shouted, but everyone was too busy travelling to catch her. And, with a job at last, she was happy.

In the evening she scavenged for food in another bin.

'On the run?' asked a black and tan bitch with a scar down her side.

'I'm controlling the monsters,' Misty replied.

'All humans are monsters,' her companion said. 'See that scar. Boys cut me open for fun.'

'The monsters stop when I tell them,' Misty continued. 'They hiss and spit and growl, but I'm in control.'

'I've got puppies,' the other dog said, 'hidden in an old drain. I don't want the humans to find them.'

'Got to go. I hear a monster coming,' said Misty as she finished a half-chewed bun with lipstick on it. 'The monsters carry humans in their stomachs.'

She ran back to the station where she stayed until midnight, although after nine the trains were few and far between. Then she drank from a puddle before sleeping in her hollow. It rained all night and she woke shivering, but when she returned to the station excitement kept her warm, despite a cold wind blowing down the railway lines.

Hungry again at noon, she went back to the bins in search of food, and came upon a group of little children walking two-by-two to a playground. She started circling them – although she longed most of all to herd them into a group – but the teacher shut the playground gate in her face.

'Go home, dog,' she said.

Then Misty returned to the station, and the ticket collector shouted: 'There she is. That's the dog.' And a uniformed man from the RSPCA crouched down and held out a piece of meat.

'Here little dog. Come here!'

His voice was kind, but his clothes reminded Misty of the policemen who had arrested Mick, so she turned away. Now, as she heard the next train coming, she stepped over the yellow line which nobody was supposed to cross, and, as she did so, the man grabbed her collar from behind and slipped a rope round her neck. 'Good girl,' he crooned, dragging her out of the station.

That night Misty slept in a kennel, her stomach full of

good food, and next morning, after a vet had examined her, she was put in a run with Bingo, a cross-bred terrier.

'Calm down, collie, you've got to look your best, so you'll find a good owner,' Bingo said. 'It's a pity you're so thin and they may not like those black spots on your muzzle. And surely your ears belong to a German Shepherd dog? People like the pure-breds. Why do you keep jumping in the air?'

'My legs make me do it,' Misty panted.

'Well stop them. You collies are all crazy,' Bingo said.

Next day the black and tan bitch was brought in with her puppies, but, although Misty barked, she had no chance to speak to her. After a week Misty became available for a new owner. The visiting children all liked her, but their parents were put off by her wild leaping in the air. Others commented on her looks.

'She's not a *real* border collie,' one complained.

'Those ears! She looks like a shirt which has come out of the wash grey instead of white.'

'She's got a bit of whippet in her,' another said.

'Too neurotic,' a third commented. 'Look, she can't stand still.'

Bingo was soon adopted by a man in a cap, and a sad greyhound was put in with Misty.

'My owners dumped me on a motorway when I couldn't win races any more,' she groaned. 'Oh, how I long to live in a house like other dogs!'

'Look anyone you fancy straight in the eye and wag your tail,' suggested Poppy, a sprightly cross-bred spaniel from the next run. 'I'm hoping to charm a sensible middle-aged woman with strong shoes. Take my advice, turn your back on anyone in high heels. They won't take you for proper walks.'

'What are proper walks?' asked Misty.

'Across fields and through woods.'

'I've never seen fields,' Misty said.

Soon a middle-aged woman chose Poppy and a kindly old man the greyhound.

'She's been raced, but she won't need a lot of exercise, greyhounds don't, not like that one.' The kennel girl, pointed at Misty. 'Collies can't stand being cooped-up.'

Morag, a white West Highland Terrier, now joined Misty.

'Do stop jumping,' she said. 'I'm a quiet little body, unless there are cats or rabbits around, and you get on my nerves.'

'Can't, legs won't,' panted Misty.

Then suddenly the weather grew very hot. The dogs lay stretched out all day in their runs, and even Misty felt tired.

She was lying on her belly, her spotted forelegs crossed elegantly in front of her when the fair-haired Mancrofts came looking for an abandoned or ill-treated dog.

'What about this one?' asked Mrs Mancroft, in her slightly refined voice. 'Isn't she lovely? – silver and white. And such style. She's like an ornament. She could be a painting in an Egyptian tomb.' As she spoke Mrs Mancroft imagined the wonderful, still Misty gracing her spotless living room.

'Yes, yes!' cried eleven-year-old Amelia, dancing up and down. 'She's pretty.'

Then Misty sprang to her feet, put her muzzle through the bars and touched Amelia's hand.

'She's very sweet-tempered, but she needs a large garden,' the kennel girl said. 'You had better come to the office. They will want all your particulars.'

Half an hour later Misty was in a car, running from side to side on the back seat, as she tried to control all the vehicles they passed on a motorway.

'Oh dear, she seems terribly wild. I hope we haven't made a dreadful mistake,' said Mrs Mancroft.

The Mancrofts' smart, deep-carpeted house was in the country next to a farm, whose fields led up to the moors.

'So you chose a working collie, then,' said Thomas, the rugged-faced farmer, as they let Misty run in the garden. 'She moves well.'

'We've called her Gemini,' Mrs Mancroft replied, 'because the star of Gemini is in ascendancy today. Gemma for short.'

It was cooler now and Gemma's legs took her across the lawn, and over a fence into a field of bullocks; they took her up a heather clad hill and down again, and then round and round the bullocks, while Mrs Mancroft called, 'Gem, Gemma, Gemini.'

'I'll whistle,' Thomas said. 'Collies come best to a whistle.' And he was right, for the moment he whistled she came, leaping back over the fence like a gazelle.

'My, doesn't she move!' he said.

Amelia caught Gemma, took her in the house and gave her a bowl of water and a plate of meat with biscuit meal. In the evening she took Gemma for a walk round the garden on a lead where, thinking of the bullocks, she pulled terribly. Afterwards Mr Mancroft, back from a day in the office, said 'Why on earth didn't you choose something little and sweet like a King Charles Spaniel?' while Gemma barked at him for the twentieth time to throw a ball she had placed at his feet. 'For heaven's sake, she's never still.'

In the morning when he found Gemma had used the kitchen as a lavatory, he told off his wife for not asking whether she was house trained.

Amelia took Gemma for a walk on a lead before going to school. Then Mr and Mrs Mancroft went to work. Shut in the house, Gemma barked until her throat was sore. Then Thomas, who kept a key for the Mancrofts, came and let her out. He took her up on the moors with his old collie,

Bess, and Gemma ran until she could run no more, and on the way down she circled the bullocks again.

When Mrs Mancroft came back at lunch time from her job, she had already decided she must return Gemma to the Dogs' Home, but Thomas forestalled her.

'That's a great dog, you've got,' he said, 'a real working collie, bred to run till she drops. But she needs to be out and about, controlling animals. I reckon all her life she's been a square peg in a round hole.'

'She's dirty in the house. I was going to take her back,' Mrs Mancroft said.

'No, don't do that,' Thomas said. 'She'll never be any good in a town. Her job's out with the cattle. I reckon way back one of her forebears was crossed with a German Shepherd to give stamina and probably at some time with a greyhound, to give speed. She's not a show dog, but she'll be great on the moors. My Bess is getting old and she and I could train Gemma to take her place. Dogs learn from each other. In six months she'll be champion, and clean in the house, too.'

And so it was. When Gemma wasn't looking after the sheep and bullocks, she bossed and played with Thomas's children who were all under five and, because she was a collie, she knew she must be especially gentle with little Pete who was only eighteen months old.

Two years later Mick saw her on television performing in sheepdog trials. He was in prison at the time, and Tracey and her mother watched her, too, from their flat. But none of them was sure she was the dog they knew as Misty, because as she herded the sheep, she seemed so calm and self-assured.

'And Misty,' Tracey's mother said, 'was nutty as a fruit cake.'

goodbye, friends

rachel anderson

For his birthday Daniel was given two gerbils in a blue cage.

'Wow, Mum!' he said. He was really pleased. He'd always wanted an animal all of his own. The dog belonged mostly to his big brother, Barry.

'Rats?' said his Gran, who had come over for the birthday tea. 'Never been very fond of rats, you know.'

'Not rats really,' said Daniel. 'Look, they're very sweet. And they won't bite if you hold them gently.'

His Gran still wasn't too keen on touching them.

At the library, Daniel's mum helped him choose a book so that he could learn all about looking after gerbils.

The pair were a male and a female. 'So they're probably going to breed,' said Daniel.

Daniel cared for the male and the female gerbil according to the instructions he read in the library book. He felt that they liked belonging to him. Each week, he spent his pocket money on a packet of gerbil food. It was a mixture of different seeds and grains. The gerbils always picked out the black and white striped sunflower seeds and ate those first.

Soon, the male would eat from Daniel's hand. The female was more timid. Both gerbils slept most of the day while Daniel was at school. They were much livelier in the evening. Then, he let them out of their cage and they leaped and frisked around on the bedroom floor while Daniel sat quietly, watching them.

He always blocked up the gap under the door with football socks and stuck a notice on the outside to warn his brother.

BEWARE!! GERBILS AT PLAY
PLEASE KNOCK BEFORE ENTERING.

Sometimes Barry sat and watched too, but he usually preferred playing football outside with the dog.

After six weeks, there was still no sign that the gerbils were going to breed. Daniel's mum said,

'Why not have a word with Ted?' Ted was Mum's brother. 'He might have some advice.'

Uncle Ted was a vet who travelled round the county visiting farms. Daniel rang him up and asked for advice.

Uncle Ted said, 'I'm more of an expert on pigs and dairy herds. But could be your gerbils are still too young. Or maybe, the climate's not right. They're desert creatures really. Wait and see what happens when the weather gets warmer.'

Daniel waited till after half-term. Still no young were born. Daniel rang his uncle again.

'Well, maybe they're just not feeling family minded,' Uncle Ted laughed.

So Daniel tried to enjoy playing with the gerbils instead of worrying about whether they might be going to breed.

On the first day of the Easter holidays Daniel discovered the nest. He opened the cage to give the gerbils their chopped apple. Usually, they scampered forward and seized the pieces from his hand. Today, the female seemed more timid than usual. She wouldn't leave her sleeping corner at the back of the cage. The male thumped his hind legs up and down as though warning Daniel to keep away.

And Daniel saw why. A litter of five, blind, slug-like creatures were wriggling in a mass in the gerbils' sleeping corner. They were not pretty, and they didn't look much like gerbils, but they were alive and they were real.

Quietly, Daniel closed the cage door, then raced downstairs to tell his family.

'It's happened!' he yelled. 'They've arrived. At last. It's like a miracle.'

Barry wanted to rush upstairs and take a look. But Daniel wouldn't let him. 'Not yet. Sorry,' he said. 'It says in the book they've to be left on their own so they don't get upset.'

At feeding time, he was careful not to frighten the new parents. He rubbed his fingers in the sawdust on the floor of the cage to cover the human smell of his hand. To their usual diet, he added grains of dried milk powder and vitamin drops to make sure that the female would be able to feed her young. He made sure too, that there was always enough water for her to drink.

At bedtime, he could hardly sleep for thinking about the gerbils. Now he had a whole family to care for. In the night, as well as the usual scufflings and scrapings, he was pretty sure he could hear the tiny high-pitched mewing of the young.

Daniel's patience was rewarded. Within a week, the boldest of the litter emerged from the nest and groped blindly but courageously about the cage with its little nose twitching.

Daniel sat and watched. It was so small, less than four centimetres long. In a few more days, it had changed into a perfect copy of the parents with the same long back legs, delicate whiskers, whiffling nose, and pink front paws, like miniature hands.

One by one, each of the babies emerged from the nest at the back and crawled around exploring their cage.

And they grew. Their weak wobbly hind legs grew stronger. Their bright eyes opened so they could see. They learned to use their dainty front paws to hold grains of seed, though they still returned to their mother for milk.

Daniel began to train them to step right into his cupped

hand to take titbits of food. At first, the male gerbil watched cautiously if Daniel put his hand near any of the babies. But gradually they all learned to trust him.

'You're really good with those little fellows, aren't you?' said Barry, and Daniel felt pleased and proud that his brother should admire him like this.

Then, one evening at feeding time, Daniel noticed that the boldest of the young, who was also the first to have been born, looked different. Daniel didn't yet know if it was male or female, but he always thought of it as a boy. His eyes were not twinkling as brightly as usual. His soft fur was damp, and he crouched, trembling, apart from the others.

Daniel closed the cage and ran downstairs to his mum who was busy making the supper.

'Mum, please help me,' he said. 'I think there's something wrong with one of the babies. And the parents aren't taking any notice.'

Mum stopped cooking and came up to have a look.

Very calmly, she said, 'Mmm, he does look a bit cold. We'd better try to keep him warm. But you know, Daniel, quite often, one of a litter is weaker than the others. They call it the runt. That's why mammals often have quite large litters so that some will survive even if the weakest don't.'

'But he *isn't* the weak one!' said Daniel. 'He's always been the strong one!'

Mum emptied out her sewing basket, and gave Daniel some cotton wool to line it with to make a cosy bed for the invalid, then they put the basket in a warm place in the airing cupboard.

Daniel woke early and went straight to the airing cupboard to see how the baby was.

It looked very dead. For a moment, Daniel hoped that

perhaps it was pretending, that it would open one bright eye and blink at him. It didn't. For a moment he was sure he saw it move. But it was only his own breath on the fur that made it move.

He lifted the tiny body from the sewing basket. He thought how he had never before touched a dead friend. It was stiff and cold. He carried it in the palm of his hand to his mum's room. He didn't have to say anything to explain. She put her arms round him and hugged.

'Yes, I'm afraid it must have died in the night. I'm so very sorry, darling,' she said.

That same evening, two more of the litter became ill. Daniel tried to do everything he could that was suggested in the book from the library on gerbil care. He separated them from the healthy ones, put them in the airing cupboard so they would benefit from the extra warmth they needed, he drop-fed them warmed milk.

'And we *must* get Uncle Ted round,' he said. '*He'll* know what else to do.'

Mum said, 'Daniel, Ted's a specialist in dairy herds, not small domestic pets.' But she rang his number anyway and got through to him on his mobile phone. He was visiting a farm only a few miles away.

He arrived in his big muddy wellies and his warm scruffy jacket. Mum gave him a cup of tea straight away, and Daniel brought down the dead gerbil for him to inspect, then showed him the other two sick ones in the sewing basket. Uncle Ted looked at them very carefully without disturbing the cotton wool.

'It looks to me as though you're giving them just the right treatment,' he said.

'But what's wrong with them?'

'Could be a virus of some kind.'

'I keep their cage really clean.'

'Small mammals can catch an infection like pneumonia very easily, just like human babies. But keep your hopes up, Danny, I expect they'll pull through.'

They didn't. Within a week, the two in the sewing basket died, then another fell ill. Soon, only one of the litter was left.

Daniel watched it leaping around the cage with its parents. It looked bright-eyed, active and healthy. It fed well from its mother's milk. It took sunflower seeds from Daniel's hand. He felt that he loved this small survivor more than the others, perhaps more than he had even cared for the parent gerbils.

Each day after school, Daniel rushed straight up to his room and stayed there, sitting close by the gerbils' cage to make sure everything was all right. As long as he was right there, he hoped that the small survivor would be safe.

But one morning when he woke, he heard no squeaking from inside the cage, only the scrabbling of the adults. The last of the babies lay dead in the sawdust. Daniel didn't even bother to pick it up. He closed the cage door and crawled back into bed. He pulled the duvet up over his head and he howled. It felt as though the whole world had ended.

Barry heard Daniel's sobbing. He climbed down from the top bunk. He asked Daniel what the matter was, even though he'd guessed. He tried to talk to him but Daniel didn't answer. So Barry went and got their mum and told her what had happened.

Mum brought Daniel a mug of hot tea to drink in bed.

'Drink up, Danny. Two sugars. Then you'll feel a bit better.'

But Daniel felt so sick he couldn't even touch it.

'Why did it have to happen?' he wept. 'What did I do wrong? If only I'd looked after them better.'

'You didn't do anything wrong, Daniel. It's not your fault,' his mum said. 'You did everything right. Remember how Uncle Ted said you cared for them so well.'

Daniel lay humped in bed all morning. He didn't ever want to speak to anyone ever again.

In the afternoon, Mum came up with a cheese and pickle sandwich. 'Come on, Daniel, it's a really lovely day. You have a bite to eat and then get up and we'll all go into town and look for those new trainers for you and Barry.'

'Shopping?' cried Daniel. 'How can I even think about shopping at a time like this?' He turned away and pulled the duvet back up over his head.

Later, Barry came up. 'I know what, Danny, you get dressed and I'll give you a game of football. You can play in goal. I'll let you borrow my best football shirt if you like.'

But Daniel just stayed in bed all afternoon. He couldn't even eat any supper. In fact, he was so unhappy that, for the first time ever, he forgot to feed the adult gerbils. Luckily, Barry remembered and did it for him.

Next morning, when Daniel first woke, it seemed like any ordinary day in the holidays, until he remembered. Today, instead of feeling sad, he was angry, with everybody.

'They were only babies!' he yelled at his mum, almost as though it was her fault. 'They never even had a chance!' He felt angry at the adult gerbils too.

'And those parents, look at them!' he shouted. 'They haven't even noticed. They don't even care.'

The male and female were scrabbling about on the floor of the cage searching for seeds they'd missed.

'They don't even *care* that their children are dead!'

Mum said, 'However much any of us care, Danny, we can't bring them back to life. There's nothing those two can do for their young now. They've just got to get on with it. But there is something important *we* must do. Today, we must bury them.'

She found an empty chocolate box. She lined it with paper tissues, and then with green leaves picked from the garden. Barry helped her. Daniel watched. Into the box, Mum and Barry carefully placed the five little bodies, each wrapped in another tissue.

Barry went and fetched the spade from the shed and dug a hole at the end of the lawn.

'Just here. See, they'll be under the shade of the silver birch tree,' he said.

Mum picked a posy of flowers.

Daniel didn't do anything. He just stood and watched.

Barry placed the box carefully into the hole in the ground and filled it in again. It wasn't a very big hole. Then he put the square of green turf back on top, then he said a sort of a prayer.

'We're all here together and thinking about these baby gerbils and are glad that they've been part of our family, even if it wasn't very long. We've all had an interesting time sharing their short but busy lives.'

Mum said, 'Amen,' and laid her flowers on top of the green turf.

Then they all went in for breakfast and Daniel managed half a piece of toast and a cup of milk. Mum was right. Now that the babies had been properly buried, he did feel a bit less unhappy though he still cried himself to sleep that night.

At the weekend, Gran came over for tea.

She always brought some nice treat for Barry and Daniel. This time, it was chocolate eggs.

'I'm ever so sorry to hear about your poor little baby rats, Danny,' she said.

Daniel nodded and sniffed. He didn't feel like reminding her that they were really called gerbils.

Gran said, 'It looks like you've got a soft spot for animals. D'you remember my little Bertie?'

'Sort of.' Daniel could dimly remember a time, long ago even before he'd started school, when Gran had always had a little white dog with her.

'D'you know, when Bertie died, I was so upset I thought I'd *never* stop missing him. I still think about him every day. But I miss him in a different way now. I expect you'll feel the same. Will you show me where they're buried?'

Daniel nodded and led the way down the garden. He was glad to show Gran because then he didn't have to talk. It was talking about the gerbils that hurt.

'Oh my! what a pretty place to be buried!' said Gran. 'You must have loved them a lot to have made such a splendid grave.' Daniel knew that it wasn't him who'd made the gerbils' grave look so pretty, but Barry and Mum.

Gran said, 'I hope that's what you're thinking of doing for me.'

'For *you*?' said Daniel, surprised. 'But you're not even old.'

'Not yet. But every living creature has to die one day. And we can never quite know when it'll be. When my time comes, I hope you and your mum, and Barry, and Uncle Ted, will make sure I get a really nice grave, with some flowers on it.'

'I'll miss you when you die,' said Daniel.

'Of course you will, Danny. But I hope that won't mean you feel you have to cry every day for the rest of your life. I'd much rather you remember all the happy things we did together. I hope you'll want to get on with living your life.'

It seemed strange to Daniel to be talking to her now about a time when she wouldn't be alive any more.

He thought, I'll always remember this moment standing here under the tree.

But instead of making him sad, it made him feel pleased.

Gran said, 'I've often thought you might end up a vet like your Uncle Ted. Always had a kindness with living creatures, did Ted, even as a boy. By the way, I brought along another little something for you, Danny.' She rummaged in her shopping bag and brought out a plant in a pot. It had green leaves and small pink flowers.

'It's a pink primula. I thought it'd be nice to put it in the grass there, on top of the burial place. I asked your Mum and she says that's fine. It'll flower again this time next year as well.'

So Daniel fetched a trowel from the shed and he and Gran planted the pink primula by the silver birch tree. Then they heard Mum calling from the kitchen that tea was ready.

Daniel took Gran's hand, and as they went in together he couldn't help himself from skipping along beside her.

fred's revenge

elizabeth pewsey

A crash.

A cloud of black, choking dust.

An eerie scratching, scrabbling sound. And two ferocious eyes glaring out of the blackness. Terrified eyes.

'It's a bird,' said Nick, going over to the chimney. 'Look.'

Tim, now that his heart had stopped thumping with fright, looked. It was indeed a bird, a gawky heap of black feathers.

'It's hurt a wing,' said Nick, after a quick inspection. 'I'd better put it out of its misery.'

'No,' said Tim. 'Don't.'

'If it can't fly, it will die anyway,' said Nick. 'It's kinder, Tim, really it is.'

'No,' said Tim. 'I'll look after him. It'll get better if he rests it. I'll put him in a box, and look after him. Just for a few days.'

'Okay,' said Nick. 'But remember, we're leaving at the end of the week.'

'I know,' said Tim with a sigh. He had been ecstatic when his much older brother had invited him to Ireland to help clean up the cottage which he had bought for the fishing.

'Cottage?' said Tim's mother. 'Bog hovel more like.'

'Ah,' said Nick. 'If Tim comes over for a few weeks, and we do some work on it, then it won't resemble a bog hovel at all. And I can rent it out to other keen fishing types, and make enough money to pay for it.'

'You should have used that money to put down a deposit on a flat somewhere,' said his mother. It was an old argument, and Nick was much happier with his dilapidated cottage in the wilds of Kerry than he would have been with a bijou residence in England.

Tim had enjoyed every minute of his time there. Best summer holidays ever, he thought as he helped dig a new cesspit, sloshed paint on walls and held nails, hammers, screwdrivers and pots of glue for Nick while he assembled the flat-pack kitchen he had brought over from England.

Nick was none too pleased at the mess the bird had brought down the chimney, sending billows of soot and twigs and dirt over his newly decorated living-room.

'I'll clean it up,' said Tim. 'When I've found a box for Fred here.'

'Fred?'

'Yes, I think he looks like a Fred.'

The bird was struggling desperately to get away from Nick's firm hold. It was clearly not in a very good state, although it still tried to give Nick's hand a peck or two.

'It's only a baby,' said Tim, taking it and putting it in a box.

'What do you think it will eat?'

'Give it those scraps off the lamb bone,' said Nick. Privately, he thought the bird wouldn't last the night, not the way its eyes were glazing over from shock and its injury.

It was Nick who got a shock next morning when he came yawning down to the kitchen to be greeted by indignant squawks and thumps from the box.

Tim burst in through the back door. 'He's alive,' he said happily.

'I can see,' said Nick. 'Best give him some water and something more to eat.'

'I have,' said Tim. 'I found him some slugs for his breakfast.'

'Revolting,' said Nick. 'I think I'll stick to toast.'

The next few days passed in a flurry of last-minute jobs, interspersed with snatched hours of fishing and, in Tim's case, bathing in the chilly water of the river which ran past the cottage on the last stage of its long journey to the sea.

And scrawny black Fred still lived. Lived and thrived.

'That's the noisiest bird I ever heard,' said Nick. 'His wing is just about healed, I'd say. We'd best let him go now.'

'Must we?' said Tim. 'Don't you think he needs to be really strong? I mean, just a bit more food would be good for him.'

'I think that bird eats more than we do,' grumbled Nick. 'We're off the day after tomorrow, though, so you'll have to resign yourself to losing your feathered friend.'

Tim had other ideas. Fred was turning out to be surprisingly tame. When Tim took him out of his box, he made no effort to escape, or even to peck at Tim, but instead sidled unsteadily along the edge of the box, his head on one side, looking at Tim with a merry, beady eye.

Tim, on his hands and knees by the bird, looked him straight in the eye and made him a promise. 'We're friends, you and me, Fred. So we'll stick together. I'm not going to leave you here. I know your wing's better, but I don't think it's perfect yet. I bet the other birds will have a go at you if I let you loose. And if they don't, some cat will get you because you can't fly out of reach quickly enough. What do you think? Do you mind leaving Ireland and coming back with me? It's just as wet there, I can tell you.'

'Caw,' said Fred.

'No,' said Nick. 'No and no and no. We are not taking that bird back with us.'

'If we can't take him, then I'm staying.'

'Don't be silly, Tim.'

'I mean it.'

And he did mean it, and Nick saw that he meant it.

'And I'll ring Mum and tell her why.'

'Oh, all right, then. But I tell you what, I'm not bringing you here again, it's far too much trouble.'

Tim merely grinned; Nick had been threatening to exclude him from treats for years. He never meant it.

'Thanks, Nick,' he said. 'I'll go down to Kelly's store and get a basket.' And I'll need to find some straw to line Fred's box, he thought, as he hared off down the track.

'You've got to be comfortable,' he whispered to the bird as he fastened down the top of the box. 'We've got a long way to go.'

'Better make sure that wretched bird's got enough to eat,' said Nick as they packed the car. 'And he'll hold us up at customs, we'll have to declare him on the way out.'

'Whatever for?'

'Exporting livestock, he counts as livestock, I suppose. Anyhow, I'm not risking it. I can't afford a fine, quite apart from the hassle if we get stopped.'

The customs man looked up as they stopped the car. 'What have you got, then?' he said without interest.

'A bird,' said Nick, pulling the box out of the back of the car and plonking it on the counter.

'Hen? Game bird? Parrot?' asked the man, looking even more bored.

'None of those,' said Nick. 'It's a wild bird, some kind of crow. It fell down the chimney and …'

'Let's have a look,' said the man, pulling open the top of the box. There was a great screech and a yell as he snatched his finger away. Blood streamed from a nasty gash about the knuckle.

'Wild bird!' he said furiously. 'You're telling me. Get that creature out of here.'

'Aren't there any forms to fill in?' asked Tim innocently.

'Clear off!' said the man.

'You won't be popular with Mum if that bird bites her,' said Nick as he steered the car off the boat at Pembroke Dock.

'It's not "that bird",' said Tim. 'It's Fred, and he won't bite her. He only attacked the man at customs because he poked him. It was a stupid thing to do.'

'I'll give Mum a ring when we stop for petrol, tell her we'll be home for supper,' said Nick. 'And that we've got a bad-tempered black bird in tow.'

'Mum will like Fred,' said Tim firmly.

Tim was right. Mum did. 'Good gracious,' she said, as Tim carefully opened the cardboard box, and she peered inside. 'What a sharp pair of eyes.'

'Out you come, Fred,' said Tim. 'He's quite tame, really. I couldn't leave him behind, Mum, now could I?'

'No, of course not. He's not to go into your bedroom, though, Tim, I absolutely forbid that. He can live in the shed by the garage.'

Tim lived in a village. It wasn't a big village, but it had a small village shop, and a pub, and a village school where Tim had gone until he was eleven.

'I never heard of a really tame crow,' said Mum. 'I should think once his wing has completely healed, you'll have to set him free.'

'He won't want to go,' said Tim confidently.

'And you must make sure that Hector doesn't get him.'

Hector was the cat; a smooth, sleek, cunning cat. He was full of affection and purrs at home, especially at the sight of a tin-opener. Once in the great outdoors, he turned into a dangerous stalker and killer.

'I don't know what I shall do if he turns up with Fred dripping from his jaws,' she said in worried tones to Nick.

'I shouldn't worry,' said Nick. 'That bird can look after itself.'

Nick was quite right. It took no time at all for Hector to

suss out Fred's whereabouts, and he immediately put him on the menu for lunch. Tail down, tummy barely an inch off the ground, Hector wormed his way into the shed. One pounce, and Fred would be gone.

A minute later there was a terrible yowl, and Hector streaked out of the shed, his tail bottle-brushed to an absurd size. He shot down the garden and into the undergrowth by the fence, not to be seen again for several hours.

Mum was impressed. 'I don't think Hector will go near Fred again,' she said. 'I wonder what he did.'

'Screeched and flapped his wings and headed for Hector's eyes, I should think,' said Tim. 'I'm proud of you, Fred,' he told him. 'There aren't many birds could get the better of Hector.'

'I think Fred's an unusual bird,' said Tim's mum.

'Bit of a hooligan, I wouldn't be surprised,' said Nick, as he threw his bag into the back of his car. His holiday was over, and he was going back to work.

'Hooligan!' said Tim indignantly as Nick roared off through the village. 'Why, Fred's very well-behaved. He only went for Hector because Hector wanted to eat him. Wouldn't you defend yourself?'

'Yes, he's normally very well-behaved,' agreed Tim's mum.

That was before Fred met the vicar. It was on his first journey out into the village. Tim had been training him to sit on his shoulder, and now, when Tim held out a hand, Fred hopped on to his wrist and marched up to perch on his shoulder. Tim had an old jumper with leather patches on the shoulder, and that protected him against Fred's claws. So when Mum asked him to pop down into the village, he thought he'd take Fred with him.

Mum didn't notice what Tim was up to. 'Now, where did

I put that other letter?' she said. 'Here we are. Two first-class stamps for those, Tim. And go into the church on your way back and put this notice up in the porch.'

'Okay,' said Tim.

All went well on the outward trip. Tim got the stamps from the machine outside the shop and posted the letters. Fred, who was very interested in the postbox, insisted on poking his head inside to see what was going on. Then Tim and Fred wandered up the path that led to the church. Fred watched as Tim pinned the notice on the wall. Birds sang, insects buzzed, butterflies flitted among the old gravestones. It was a peaceful scene.

Until the vicar appeared from inside the church.

'It wasn't my fault, mum,' said Tim a little later. 'The vicar was wearing that long black thing ...'

'His cassock,' said Mum.

'Whatever,' said Tim. 'And it frightened Fred. Maybe he thought the vicar was giant crow.'

'Tim!' said his mother warningly.

'Well, he does look a bit sinister, and Fred's only a baby, really.'

'Some baby,' said Mum, having had to calm down an irate vicar who had a long deep scratch on his cheek, and a nasty chunk of bird mess all down one sleeve. 'If he does it again, Tim, he'll have to go. It's a small community here, and we can't have the vicar attacked every time Fred catches sight of him. In fact, I think it would be best if you didn't take Fred out and about. He can't get up to much mischief here.'

Famous last words. Fred took exception to the postman, the person who came to read the meter and the oil delivery man. He particularly didn't like the oil delivery man.

'Blimey,' the man said, retreating to his tanker cab. 'What's up with that bird?'

'I don't think he likes the flash on your uniform,' said Tim.

'Blimey,' he said again. 'I'm not coming back here. Not with that great black crow attacking me.'

'Oh, Tim,' said Mum. 'We need oil for the heating.'

'They'll send someone else,' said Tim optimistically.

The letter came two days later, regretting that the firm could not risk harm to their employees by asking them to deliver to a house where a Dangerous Bird was on the loose.

'You're in disgrace, Fred,' said Tim, tweaking his feathers in the way he liked.

'That bird's enormous,' said Nick when he came down for the weekend. 'I'm sure he shouldn't be that big.'

'It's all the food Tim gives him,' said Mum. 'He seems very healthy; I'm sure he'd be fine if we took him to the woods.'

'Mum,' said Tim reproachfully. 'He hasn't attacked anyone for days. See how friendly he is with Nick.'

'Thanks very much,' said Nick, looking at Fred's little offering on his shoulder. 'Are you doing a wash, Mum?'

Nick was upstairs, getting dressed for the village hop.

'Nick,' Mum called up the stairs. 'Aren't you ready? You're going to be late, it's ten to eight.'

'I can't find my cufflinks,' said Nick, clattering down the stairs.

'They're on the window-sill in your room.'

'They aren't,' said Nick. 'The box is there, but no cufflinks.'

'That's strange,' said Mum. 'Did you take them out?'

'Yes, to polish them,' said Nick. 'But I'm sure I put them back.'

A search of Nick's room and then the rest of the house

failed to turn up Nick's cufflinks, and in the end he had to go off without them.

Next day, Nick took Tim down to the village pub. Fred went too. 'I'll be sitting outside,' said Tim when Nick saw him on Tim's shoulder. 'He hasn't attacked anyone recently, I told you. And he loves crisps. He'll be fine.'

'Where's Fred?' said Nick, coming out with a beer for himself and a coke for Tim.

'He flew off,' said Tim, in a worried voice. 'I went to look for him, but I can't see him anywhere.'

'Cheer up,' said Nick, privately hoping that Fred had gone for good. Vain hope, he told himself, as Fred landed on the table in front of them with a friendly caw of greeting.

'Fred, where have you been?' said Tim, as Fred pecked at the bag of crisps.

After that, Fred went about a lot with Tim. He often went off now, but Tim didn't worry any more, because he always came back.

'Wonder where he goes,' said Tim, squinting into the sunlight as Fred flapped up into the air, gave a few swoops, circled and then flew off.

'Hunting, I expect,' said Mum. 'Tim, I've lost a silver earring. You haven't seen it, have you?'

'It'll turn up,' said Tim.

'Can you come to the village with me?' went on Mum. 'I have to collect two boxes of tomatoes, and you can help carry them.'

'I suppose so,' said Tim.

Fred joined them as they walked into the village, landing on Tim's shoulder with a thud and his customary squawk of greeting.

'Where've you been?' said Tim, ruffling his feathers.

'There's Susanna,' said Mum as they walked past the pub

garden. Susanna was Nick's girlfriend. 'Let's join her for a coffee.'

'No, let's not,' said Tim. Yak, yak, yak, he thought.

'You can have some crisps,' said Mum. 'Hello, Susanna.'

'Hi,' said Susanna, eyeing Fred.

'This is Fred,' said Tim. 'He's an Irish crow.'

The sound of angry voices came out of the pub window. 'I tell you, there are only a dozen left.'

'What's up?' said Mum.

'Someone's pinching the teaspoons,' said Susanna, stirring her coffee with one of the few remaining spoons. 'It's getting expensive, replacing them.'

'If I catch whoever's nicking them, I'll kick them into the next county,' shouted Harry, the landlord.

'Tim,' said Susanna. 'Are you sure Fred's a crow?'

Tim watched in astonishment as Fred, eyes bright and fixed on the teaspoon on Susanna's saucer, sidled across the table. Then there was a quick swoop, and swish of wings, and Fred was gone.

The three of them looked at each other.

'I think Fred's a very big jackdaw,' said Susanna.

Harry came roaring out of the pub. 'I saw that. I saw him. It's that dratted bird of yours, Tim. He's been taking all my teaspoons. Why, he must have been in through the kitchen window and lifted them. Just wait till I get my hands on him. I'll wring his shiny black neck, so I will.'

Tim leapt to his feet. 'Fred's a pet,' he said.

'I don't think you can train jackdaws not to steal. They all do it,' said Susanna.

'Calm down, Harry,' said Mum, trying not to laugh. 'Of course you wouldn't harm Fred.'

'Oh, wouldn't I just?'

'What we've got to do,' said Susanna, leading the way

back to the cottage at a brisk pace, 'is find where Fred's hiding all his loot.'

It didn't take long. Tim pulled at a box which was resting on a beam in the shed, and a shower of teaspoons came tumbling down around his ears. As well as the vicar's silver pen and a cache of shiny coins. 'Oh, Fred,' said Tim. 'You thief.'

They found Nick's cufflinks, Mum's earring, and several of their own best teaspoons behind the fridge.

'Fred will have to go, Tim,' said Mum in a worried voice. 'He's obviously a kleptomaniac. And I really think Harry might take a pot-shot at him with that rook gun of his.'

Tim went pale. 'He couldn't shoot Fred.'

'Hi, Mum,' said Nick. 'How's things? Where's Tim?'

'At the zoo,' said Mum.

'In a cage?'

'No, but Fred is,' said Mum. 'Susanna knew this zoo with a big aviary; she said they'd want Fred, because he so tame and such a character.'

'Cheer up, Tim,' said Nick later. 'Fred will be happy there, and he'd have got up to mischief once you were back at school. I'm going back to Ireland for a week. Coming?'

'You bet,' said Tim.

'Only this time,' said Mum, 'no wildlife!'

dolphin story collections

chosen by **wendy cooling**

1 top secret

stories to keep you guessing by rachel anderson, andrew matthews, jean richardson, leon rosselson, hazel townson and jean ure

2 on the run

stories of growing up by melvin burgess, josephine feeney, alan gibbons, kate petty, chris powling and sue vyner

3 aliens to earth

stories of strange visitors by eric brown, douglas hill, helen johnson, hazel townson and sue welford

4 go for goal

soccer stories by alan brown, alan durant, alan gibbons, michael hardcastle and alan macdonald

5 wild and free

animal stories by rachel anderson, geoffrey malone, elizabeth pewsey, diana pullein-thompson, mary rayner and gordon snell

6 weird and wonderful

stories of the unexpected by richard brassey, john gatehouse, adèle geras, alison leonard, helen mccann and hazel townson

7 timewatch

stories of past and future by stephen bowkett, paul bright, alan macdonald, jean richardson, francesca simon and valerie thame

8 stars in your eyes

stories of hopes and dreams by karen hayes, geraldine kaye, jill parkin, jean richardson and jean ure

9 spine chillers

ghost stories by angela bull, marjorie darke, mal lewis jones, roger stevens, hazel townson and john west

10 bad dreams

horror stories by angela bull, john gatehouse, ann halam, colin pearce, jean richardson and sebastian vince